IN THE SPACE BETWEEN

IN THE SPACE BETWEEN

The Poetry of Embodiment

Tias Little

©2024 by Tias Little and Prajna Yoga
All Rights Reserved.

The characters and events portrayed in this book are fictitious. Any similarity to real persons, living or dead, is coincidental and not intended by the author. No part of this book may be reproduced, or stored in a retrieval system, or transmitted in any form or by any means, electronic, mechanical, photocopying, recording, or otherwise, without express written permission of the publisher.

ISBN-13: 9798218403614

Designed by: Patricia Cousins
Printed in the United States of America

prajnayoga.com

For Surya
whose heart burns longest,
strongest and brightest,
forever loving, and radiant

Space always reduced me to silence.

—Jules Valles

CONTENTS

Introduction	*xi*	The Poetry of Embodiment
EARTH	*1*	
	2	Savasana
	3	Sanctify the Space Within
	4	Kundalini
	5	Rest Horizontal
	6	Setting Down the Great Burden
	7	Ashes to Ashes
	8	On Bone
	9	Firm Back/Soft Front
	10	In the Mountains of New Mexico
WATER	*11*	
	12	The Droplet
	13	First Pulse
	14	Full Fathom Five
	15	Getting Out of Your Own Way
	16	Condensation
	17	Working with the Inner Weather
	18	Spring Melt
	19	Unthawing
	20	Yoking to the Creative Source
	21	Soaking Inside
	22	Morning Tea
	23	Pulse of the Ancient Tide
	24	The Now of the Tao
	25	Learning to Let Go
FIRE	*26*	
	27	The Unforgettable Fire
	28	The Gloaming Hour
	29	The Light Within the Dark
	30	Revelation
	31	Lord of the Dance
	32	The Spark of Death
	33	I Remember This Feeling
	34	December Full Moon
	35	The Zen of Oz

AIR 36
	37	Savasana II
	38	Savor the Silence
	39	Call of Solitude
	40	The Whisper of God
	41	Heed the Call
	42	The Breather's Breath
	43	This Very Moment
	44	The Spirit of Repetition
	45	The Spirit of Play
	46	No Separation
	47	The Trap of Entitlement

SPACE 48
	49	In the Space Between
	50	Consecrate the Space Within
	51	Circular Breathing
	52	Giant Earplugs
	53	Where the Infinite and the Finite Meet
	54	Silent Sky
	55	Believe in Nothing
	56	Tent Top
	57	Black Crow
	58	Kudos to the Unspeakable
	59	End of the Year
	60	It's This Simple
	61	Be as You Are
	62	Feast Today

In Gratitude
64

Introduction

The Poetry of Embodiment

As a devoted student of the internal arts, I have spent countless hours on the mat exploring both depths and surfaces of my body. In my pursuit, I realized that the body is never fixed, never static, but like the constant sway of the ocean, lifts and swirls, rises and retreats. The sands of bodily tissue are moved by the currents of time, formed, and reformed by life circumstance.

Through movement practice, we participate in ongoing circulatory change. In this light, we are all shapeshifters, altering the contour of our organs, glands and vessels. We shift between high tide and low tide, riding waves of breath under the persuasion of the lunar pull. We extend forward and pull back, sweep to the side, arch, churn, polish, and roll.

This collection of poems and prose explores the intersection of language, movement, anatomy, sensory awareness, and imagination. I draw heavily from my own experience in attending to the 10,000 pulses and currents that travel through my body. I speak to my own struggles on the path to make progress, to free myself from entanglements and to welcome both the mundane and the transcendent each day.

I have discovered after years of reading other poets in class, that poetic language has an alchemical effect on the connective tissues of the body. Over the years, I have selected poetry that speaks to the soul's passage and prompts nuanced and delicate shifts through the body's interior. Elevated by other poets' work, I felt called to craft my own passages to help cast light on the hidden spaces within.

Imaginative language inspires new sensations and new ways of being. Descriptive language, metaphors, and allusions leave their mark on impressionable organs and glands. Images can alter our shape—they *inform* the contours of our spine, change the tension in our gut and alter the squeeze and pump of our cardiac rhythm.

Like interior tattoos, words etch and inscribe us with beauty, aesthetic appreciation, and fresh insights. Language alters perception and in turn, perception influences our felt sense of being. The body is like a lump of clay, and words, like a sculptor's blade, can help shape, chisel, and mold us. In this way, the language of the subtle body helps awaken new sensations and new meanings.

Images and metaphors allude to a thing that, paradoxically, can never be put into words. They coax the unsuspecting listener into realms previously unimagined. They are guides that foster connection to invisible forces that have no form, shape, or size. Like a salve to a wound, they ameliorate the flesh by making it more supple and pliant. They are spirit whisperers that coax the listener to a kind of inner communion, a sensory communion.

Like pathways that lead through a series of outer gates into the inner sanctum of a temple, poetic language can lead to a kind of awakening of the soul. When beholding in our mind's eye a river, cloud, god, or grandmother, we are guided into our own rich and textured biography, replete with memories and associations.

I intend for these poems and prose pieces to be read by teachers during savasana or in meditation, to help shift the tides of breath and immerse in the ocean of being. They are meant to touch the interstitial spaces of memory and help promote an affinity to mystery. More than anything, they are meant to awaken a feeling of belonging inside.

If you offer one of these pieces to a class, provide the time and space for the aesthetic feeling to emerge, slowly circulate, and then soak in. Like tea leaves, allow time for the language to steep inside. Trust in the alchemy of the imagery, that it will provide nuanced shifts as people travel through the landscape of their own imagination.

Language can open us to awe and the wild ways of spirit. The passages that follow bid the listener away from the spell of the surface and into the depths of being. Any lasting shift must be psychosomatic. Thus, the image of the tower, the root, the serpent, or the hummingbird alters thought waves, cranial rhythms, and breath. As these images circulate through your bloodstream and fire across your nerves, I hope they will work their own kind of magic. May they summon a presence that enchants and help yoke to a spirit unconfined.

—Tias Little
Santa Fe, New Mexico
July, 2023

EARTH

Savasana

This settling is like no other.
Let your bones drop like
fallen tree limbs
now inseparable from
the dark, rich humus of the forest floor.
Let your flesh and sinews be
food for a thousand creeping lives.
Let your eyes be the light
for the tendril growth of new shoots.
Let your blood be the rivers that guide
the young salmon in migration.
Let your breath be a blanket of peace
to cover the wounds of the world.

Sanctify the Space Within

Just as the smoke of an incense stick
dissolves into space
let thoughts swirl, drift, and evaporate.
Let yourself be fanned
by the winds of breath, the winds of time.
The Buddha taught, "all that arises ceases."
Let everything come to rest.
Let the white ash of your old self
drop to the ground,
like the bones of the body of Christ,
wafer-like and fine.
Take the remains from the fire,
smear your skin,
sanctify the space within.

Kundalini

Take the spiral stairway down,
like strands of DNA revolving
right to left, left to right,
clear down to the bottom.

Enter your breath stream
in the commissure of your skull
(thalamus, pons, corpus callosum)
there you can meander for miles,
serpentine, like the longest river—
Yangtze, Ganga, Huang Ho, Sushumna.

Count to yourself slowly
...Miss-iss-i-ppi...
let the current take you
down, down, down,
sometimes swift, sometimes slow
into the holy waters of your sacrum.
Let your breath be the guide
that turns your raft
a thousand leagues under the sea.

Rest Horizontal

Do we need to keep building higher and higher?
Must we climb the rugged mountain
clambering for the stars?
I get lost in ascension and so want
nothing but mass and weight and
a thousand miles of solid ground below.

I renounce my upward striving,
and the longing to be light and lifted.
I let my proud spires fall and rest horizontal
—still, and serene—
on the broad back of *terra firma*.
Here I need not reach for heaven
or the approval of FaceTime followers.
I drop anything I don't need for the final journey home.
I let God be my ground.

And like all things at the end of time,
the flesh drops away from my bone and
the pores of my skin open.
In this dark and fertile soil
I take the company of a thousand creeping lives,
a web of invisible microbes,
stretching far and wide.
Like a winter seed,
I tuck into the earth
knowing that the season of regeneration awaits me.

Setting Down the Great Burden

The big burden we bear day in and day out is astonishing in scale. Each of us is loaded with expectations for success, weighed down with anxiety for the future, and pre-occupied by a to-do-list 108 entries long. It is like lugging a rucksack full of rocks around town. Our shoulders get sore and oh, how the upper trapezius tightens! We are so accustomed to our burden we do not realize we are hefting such a heavy load; until one day we throw it off, take a few steps back, look at the big pack stuffed to the max with fear and craving and say, "OMG, I can't believe I have been carting this thing around like a mule since second grade!" A big part of the problem is that we identify our backpack as mine —*my* thoughts, *my* agendas, *my* pleasures, *my* traumas. When you throw off your "mental luggage" it is liberating. You feel buoyant, like a levitating yogi.

Today you can inhale desert toad venom, gulp down a few magic mushrooms, or take some Vitamin K, all to help you realize that the baggage you shoulder is not the essential you. Meditation helps us to see that the weight we bear is an imposition, a presumption, really just a cumbersome add on. Your load may be a hand-me-down, inherited from someone in your family tree, or perhaps something happened to you long ago that compelled you to haul the load around with you everywhere you go.

At some point in your journey, you will have the direct experience of the pack coming off. When it drops to the ground you will feel much lighter in your bones, tendons, fascia, and joints. However, this off-loading is not easy. You may have been carting that pack around for a lifetime, possibly multiple lifetimes, so long, that it adheres to your flesh and your skin. Getting to the yoga mat helps. When you fold, twist, and lengthen, the adhesions along your back loosen.

Sometimes it happens that you cast off your pack for a time, but because you are so habituated to the *lugasana*, you hoist it right back onto your shoulders saying, "hey, this belongs to me." It takes time to see the baggage as not you and it takes practice to embody "no burden." So, try this a little bit everyday: unfasten your waist belt and chest strap, slip your arms out and drop the thing to the ground. When you unfetter your load, sense the way it frees up your fascia and makes it a hell of a lot easier to breathe.

Ashes to Ashes

I am on my back now
at the end of a long and circuitous march
across vast stretches of land —ridges, rifts, and valleys—
down stairways, hallways and kitchens.
I'm done building —raising up and tearing down.
I'm done trying to get from point A to point B.
No more straight lines here, no geometry—
the architecture of me vanished.

It's difficult to explain
and the words I form feel flimsy,
like the skeletal wings of the moth
found today between anatomy books on the top shelf in my library.

As it is said in the book of Common Prayer,
"We therefore commit this body to the ground,
earth to earth, ashes to ashes, dust to dust,"
this stitchwork of bones, flesh and sinews
will be but etchings in the loam.

The wind drops and a sudden stillness enters the room.
I can't see it, smell it, touch it, or hear it.
But they are near, like the deer on the edge of the meadow at dusk.
I feel their silent bidding for me to follow
into the black night, through the thicket of stars
—*via lactea*, the milky way—
to join the flying atoms,
the particles of prana,
that have been dancing
since the beginning of time.

On Bone

Stand in the matrix of the mother
fortified and firm,
porous and pliable,
built from ancestral saline deposits
—10,000 honeycombed cells—
buried like catacombs-
below the ancient city.

Stout like a god,
stand in the blood-well of your bones,
citadels of calcium,
pillars to the temple of your spine.

Under the weight of layers and layers of sediment,
sense the liquid ooze in your marrow,
—ilia, femoral—
aquafers of blood formed
under years of geothermal pressure,
charged with electric hum.

Go, now, higher,
up into the rafters of your skull
where the ossea are exquisite and fine
like cross-stitched lace,
delicate as dragonfly wings.

All through the night
atmospheric currents
of cerebrospinal fluid
drift beneath your sutures
—swooping upward and dipping down—
like swallows exiting the church belfry at dusk,
flying high over the town square in your dreams.

Firm Back / Soft Front

When you first wake up in the morning, take a pee and go straight to your cushion. Meditate with a firm back and soft front. With firm back be resilient, solid, and unswerving. With soft front, be permeable, receptive, and open. Sitting in the morning with firm back/soft front will give you the resolve and the fluidity to be with all that arises in the course of your day.

With a broad firm back, you have little to fear. You can trust the road you are on, be it ridden with potholes, or be it seamless and smooth. When the world goes topsy-turvy, you "have at your back" the knowing that you are always connected to a great thing, an unseen support. For behind you, you have the backing of the ancestors who didn't fret over petty things, who abandoned self-criticism and self-harm and walked a straight path.

At the same time, move through the world with a soft front. With a soft front, you are ready to encounter the new, open to ongoing discovery and surprise. With a soft front you need not put up the old guard of doubt and defense, but lean forward into the mystery and welcome the unknown. With soft front everything becomes possible.

Embodying firm back and soft front, you live a life both anchored and uplifted, steadfast, and changeable. At your back is timeless time, a perpetual presence, far bigger and wider than anything you can calculate or reason. At your front, is the split second of this very moment, forever changing, appearing, and disappearing. Put firm back and soft front into practice. Then you can pass through any gate and overcome any barrier.

In the Mountains of New Mexico

Sitting just sitting
like the body of an old pine
sprung out of rock.

This ocean mind
knows no direction
taking refuge
in the shelter of morning sky.

WATER

The Droplet

Like the giant Sequoia
let your trunk be upright and broad
your spinal column pithy,
shooting straight for the sky.
Let your eyelids be diffuse as morning mist,
and let your back skull float into the canopy on high.

Sense your brain expand with each breath
like cumulus clouds in the summer-time sky.
At the apex of your skull, a droplet
—a most exotic dew—
drips downward,
crystalline, reflective, luminous.

Suspend your awareness
in this very moment
so that you are inseparable
from the trees, the stars, the sky.

First Pulse

It all starts as a whiptail squiggle in a sea of protoplasm,
head down, bumping around blindly
while everything tremors and quakes.
Right off the bat, you start dividing like crazy
then cling for dear life to the blood rich placenta
like a solitary barnacle in a bed of sea kelp.

Can you remember the feeling of sway,
drifting in saline solution
like plankton or stardust?
Can you relive the first pulse
in the ground substance of your being
through ripples of cytoplasm,
in the hum of mitochondria,
and so inhabit the energy behind all creation?

It is not really a memory but a felt sense,
like taking a bath with your eyes closed and becoming real still,
or driving over a hill on a county road and
feeling your stomach heave before settling.
It is a memory that predates the cortex,
a return to the trilobites, the lancelets, the coelacanths.
It is a primordial pulse,
a perpetual cadence,
reverberating in you as the murmur of blood
and the tremor of nerve.

Be the ancient tide
gushing and flowing,
trickling still.
Can you feel the presence of
the ancestors surging through your veins?

Full Fathom Five

Let your bones be like black earth,
fertile and dense
the back of your skull a cache of secrets—
dreams waking and asleep.
Let your mammalian blood wash over you,
pulsing through your cranial cavities
bathing your brain in saline waters.
Let the shaft of your spine
widen like a river delta opening to the sea.

Breathe into your back
until you are taken under
—amniotic—
buoyed by currents of tidal flow.
Feel the moan and murmur
of each pulse inside
as if guided by echolocation.

Migrate off the coast of your former habit worn self,
and be a cetacean a thousand feet down,
piloting through acoustic caverns
—ethmoid, sphenoid, temporal—
be a weightless mass piloting through
millions of nautical miles.
In these depths
there is nothing but heartbeat and waves
purrs and whispers.

At last, your breath goes to naught
and you detect an old prompt,
clear as a temple bell,
calling you to the surface.
Time to come up for air.

Getting Out of Your Own Way

On the long and winding journey on the path of practice, you may finally come to the place where you realize the best thing to do is get out of your own way. At some point, you have to stop engineering your life and allow a force greater than yourself to enter.

But how to get out of your own way? Some people drink whiskey or rave dance all night. Some dive off cliffs or go on shopping sprees. Yogis go to the space between breaths, between their right side and left side, and between their back and their front. They go between the identities of male and female and the persuasive pull of sun and moon. There the mind loses its grip and the anguished heart subsides. There you can hover like a dragonfly, weightless in concentration, clear of mind. There you are neither seeking nor finding, neither making progress nor losing ground.

Thinking won't take you there and by trying to make yourself better, you only get in your own way. Don't expect to gain anything or get rid of anything. You only have to enter the space between, slip through the gap between worlds, and become part of the great unfolding.

When your mind empties, an enormity rushes in on the ebbing tide, filling every nook and cranny of your being. When the flow of the great river of *samadhi* comes, you need only yeild to its power and let it take you.

Condensation

What are the conditions outside today?
Is more suffering forecast?
At the edge of the front, warm and cold air collide
while a low-pressure system moves in.

On the wind of breath I ride
tenuous as cirrus clouds
high up the rafters of my ribs.
Particles of breath dance and swirl
—atmospheric, *pranic*, cathartic—
until the wind drops and a strange silence
settles over me, weighty, like cold mist in the valley at dawn.

The air inside is delicate as vapor
particles of prana soak my lungs
like a towel on the dewy grass
left out all night.
Breathing is mysterious, unpredictable,
at times swelling like spring snowmelt
and then stopping and standing still like a horse.

In rarefied stillness
thoughts condense into a single droplet
—a water crystal glistening and transparent—
until a lone teardrop
breaks free from the dewy surface of my eye.
And the rain falls far and wide for days.

Working with the Inner Weather

It used to be that talking about the weather was what you did to fill time, chatting with strangers or catching up on the phone with your parents. But today, talk of the weather references real time disaster —flooding, torrential rain, typhoons and raging wildfires. As we speak, there are climactic catastrophes all over the map: the Bootleg fire in Oregon, the North Rhine Westphalia flood in Germany, the Yellow River flood in Zhengzhou China. Our poor globe is experiencing eco-convulsions like never before and daily we grapple with feelings of impending doom.

In an era of constant media updates, we witness daily threats of destruction and loss as breaking stories ping our phones. For example, just the other day on a recent trip to town, the navigation system on my Subaru flashed an ominous alarm: "EMERGENCY FLASH FLOOD WARNING." Smaller text identified a weather system 100 miles off in the next county. I drove to town nerve racked and restless, anticipating that I would be consumed by a wall of water any second. This kind of menacing alert could pitch anyone into a full-blown panic. Today, no place on the planet is immune to weather seizures and convulsions. It is a threat we all live with.

However, while none of us can control the outside weather, we can regulate our internal climate. In fact, the very definition of mindfulness suggests that we watch our "mind weather." In the face of a foreboding future, we must avoid getting swept up in gales of anxiety, high-pressure systems of stress, or low-pressure systems of despair. We must track heat waves of irritation and cold fronts of hopelessness and fear. Aggravating winds can fray nerves, amp up blood pressure, and wreak havoc on digestion. Gusts of anxiety, fear, and doom result in many a sleepless night. Amidst the threat of global warming (or "global weirding" due to the wild fluctuations in climate), we could spend our days fretting and chafing, caught in a kind of "global worrying." If not careful, we become storm chasers, running headlong into vortexes of despair.

While taking precautions and being informed is imperative, doing the *worry-asana* is not. To avoid falling into sink holes of gloom, hopelessness, and fear, cultivate an unruffled heart and ready mind. Pacify the blustery winds of anxiety and dread while settling into places of relaxation and deep calm. Only then can we remain centered and resilient, ready to adapt to a changing world.

Spring Melt

Ice pack buckles in the torrent of the spring stream.
Who could stand this relentless gushing?
Its momentum shifts the contours of my mind
so that the banks through which I wander now widen
while the familiar landmarks I once knew
are washed away in the stream's shifting course.

Heading home in the falling light
my legs unthawing with each step,
I follow a sixth sense,
a kind of inner navigation
when above me, I hear the distant pump of robust wings,
a flock of migrating geese
—on a straight course—
soaring high,
headed for their summer stomping grounds.

Unthawing

In sitting today
an icy grief
condenses in my chest,
weighty and grey.
White bubbles of trapped air
suspend in my lungs
like insects frozen in amber.
I am swallowed whole by an ancient ache,
dense and thick
one that constricts and expands outward
at the same time.

Under pressure,
my heart suddenly cracks,
a kind of thwacking split,
that resounds for miles
like the woodland pond in springtime
unthawing its solid mass of ice.

And my heart bleeds
droplets of liquid gold.

Yoking to the Creative Source

Can you find a way each day to tap the creative pulse of the world? This pulse is always already inside you, and inside all sentient beings. But you don't see it or feel it. You are too busy, entranced by the litany of tasks and obligations that define you. Spellbound by the things of the world, you neglect the very source that sustains you. This source is invisible, silent, and steady. When you get on your cushion or mat, sense its iron pull, like a magnet drawing you close.

In the flow of your daily round, you need only trust its traction, follow its invisible tug, and let it flow through you. Like gravity, it will hold you to the ground while lifting you up. Mysterious, never to be seen, its perpetual presence induces every breath, triggers every thought, and prompts every action. Let your whole life be an expression of this generative force so that, like a work of art, all that you do is an ongoing act of creation.

And because the source is unlimited, each of your actions is unlimited. When you fail to realize this, blinded by your own pursuit, you become worn out and exhausted. You need not resist it or try to improve upon this great source. Only realize that you are already held, already yoked, that you belong to it, like a star fixed in the firmament of the night sky. All you need do is relinquish yourself to its oceanic pull and let it take you in its tireless sway.

Soaking Inside

You have to coax yourself to the edge
not of grit and vigor
but where you can feel a change come over you
like blue dye poured onto white cloth.
Let the sensation of serenity spread
filling every nook and cranny of your being
like making blood after a big meal,
or a grassy field drenched in morning dew.

Stop all your striving and struggle.
You need only soak into the ground substance
of your being
—synovial, gelatinous—
like the flesh of an octopus,
tasting the world through touch.

With your brain in your skin
shapeshift your bones—
be slithery, aqueous, and pliable.
When you let go of who you are
and who you think you ought to be,
you become the color of the place you are in.

Morning Tea

The morning sky is reflected
in my cup of oolong tea,
a boundless expanse
now but a slip stream
of wakefulness
travelling across space and time,
—in one gulp—
down the back of my throat.

Pulse of the Ancient Tide

The blue, blue sea
shows tireless devotion,
begotten by an unseen force
ebbing and flowing without fail,
circulating like clockwork—
and breathing.

Let its magnificent surge
cradle you in its long arms
and carry you,
not to a place of worship, want, or knowing
but to where you have always been
and already are,
in the perpetual tide
of your heart's undulating rhythm,
bobbing like a buoy in a protected bay.

Sense the amplitude of a million sea swells
rising and falling with gravity
along the willowy stalk of your spine,
a fluid cadence
as old as the breath of the gods.

From your sacrum to your skull
feel the tug of time's ancient signature
encircling your spine in a
profusion of briny mist,
drenching every pore.
When closest to the heavenly body,
at the still point of the fluctuating tide,
all that remains is wind and breath and
the taste of sea spray on your tongue.

The Now of the Tao

When you practice, remember that you are in the now wherever you are and in whatever you do. The now is constant, right at the tip of your fingers, ever productive and always available. It is eternally immanent, diurnal, with you in every breath, every passing thought, every split-second. "Just this! Just this!," exclaims the Zen master.

I tend to forget the now altogether and get caught up in plans for the future while longing for a place I imagine to be better and more enlightened than where I am now. But there is no place to get to, no "final frontier." Rather, like the Tao, all is in process, all is on its way, flowing and swirling, sometimes swift, sometimes slow, in the river of the now.

The Tao refers to the way things are. Like water, silence, technology and time, the Tao flows continuously. Never static, never fixed, all things are an ongoing expression of the Tao. You can witness the flow of the Tao in music, in a rainstorm, in the shimmer of light in the oak tree, or in the flood of emails entering your inbox. The Tao is what is arising right now as we speak. The Tao is in your DNA, your peristalsis, and cardiac rhythm. Fashioned out of the matrix of the Tao, each of us is an inescapable part of an ever-flowing stream of moments. In this way we are all verbs—becoming, morphing, transpiring. Know that you are part of the perpetually changing present. Don't imagine you are outside of it or live apart from it. Rather, trust that you are part of a great unfolding.

Learning to Let Go

I stop digging, put down my plough,
the earth will grow on without me.
I agree to talk less, read more poems
and attend to the cadence of silence inside.

From my rooftop at dusk,
the light grows weary in the Western sky,
fading like the speckled color on the back of a dying fish.
Can I trust my internal navigation device to chart my way home?
Can I relinquish custody to a grave immensity
and let its momentous strength pull me in?
Just then, I remember this Zen haiku:

The huge fish
flutter motionless below
facing the current.

Last night I dreamed a procession
came through town—a whale on the flatbed
of an eighteen-wheeler.
Ecclesiastes dressed in long robes
gestured signs of benediction.
I heard then, as I do now,
a call from the fathomless depths,
a high-pitched squeal,
like the sound of a steam train pulling out of the station.
The enormity of the ocean beckons,
an upwell of current takes me,
and I travel by echolocation
down, down, down into the depths below.

FIRE

The Unforgettable Fire

This longing dives deep in me
straight down to the seabed of my soul,
not a longing for name or riches
or the approval of others,
but for the spirit whisperer, the silent secret presence,
that rides on every breath, echoes with every thought
and resounds on every syllable.
It is a primordial yearning
—Neanderthal—
like an ember from the first fire,
still burning
as etchings and song,
and stencils of stars drawn in the night sky.
It is a passion that must never be extinguished,
but always stay with you
tucked like a brilliant bead,
in a leather pouch
against your belly for safekeeping.
Animate the light inside your dark,
give breath to the spark within you.
In the caverns of your bones
let the white flame rise upward,
glistening bright.

The Gloaming Hour

Listen till your ears burn
and the fire of your breath glows
infra-red, soaking
right through you
from skin to soul.

I have lost track of time.
I have stopped counting the days,
the hours and the minutes.
I have ceased sending and receiving too.

A stupendous silence fills me
a galaxy of space, perpetually bright
spreading like saffron dye
across the white cloth of my back.

I am led onward
by a gentle heave of breath
like the way a child rolls over in her sleep
with a sigh and a soft mutter.

A tiny flame flickers in my belly
then exhales its final want.
Something in me gets
extinguished,
like the still, silent embers from last night's fire.
It is then that an immense serenity
overtakes me,
the way the evening sun
plummets into the ocean,
leaving behind a curtain
of white light hanging over the water.

The Light Within the Dark

In a time that cracks and splinters all around,
when vile men lose their minds in pursuit of gold, oil, and fame,
when the very ground you walk trembles
from windstorms and earthquakes,
when trepidation wakes you at 3AM
and your faith in humanity is on trial,
you must do the one thing that
will save you from darkness and despair—
you must enter the cave of your heart,
breathe in the fragrance of the night,
and belong to the enormity of silence.

Stop forming so many words,
step outside the machinations of your mind
and be sustained by that which has existed since time immemorial.
Here there is nothing pressing you forward or pulling you back.
Here you are like the sky, unconfined in awareness, naked of heart.
Here the original brightness illuminates every fiber
of your being from skin to soul.
Here you need only breathe the ancient rhythm,
titrating between love and loss, grief, and joy.

When you open your eyes to the light within the dark
your love gets deeper, wider, softer, and stranger.
See through the pain of this world,
let yourself belong to it, no end in sight.

Revelation

What gets revealed today?
And must you travel to the Himalaya,
the jungles of Brazil,
fast and stand naked in front of the fire
until your heart cracks open?

For so long you have been left wanting a vision of the gods,
to hear the great roar of truth,
to be illumined by a single ray of light.
You search 'til your eyes burn
and your spine bends down from the burden.
Wringing your flesh in pursuit of the holy passion
you have been hunting angels too long…

Now it is time to stop the chase.
Drop by drop
the world reveals itself—
in a cup of morning tea,
in the surprise call from an old friend,
in the trail of raindrops
sliding down the windowpane.

Like homeopathy,
epiphanies are everywhere.
There! particles of dust
dancing in the shaft of sunlight.
There! the tangy taste of the umeboshi plum on my tongue.
There! a blanket of cloud draping over the ridgetop.

To be revealed, you need only open your front door,
step into the glow of morning light,
and with heels on solid ground,
let the 10,000 things rise up to greet you.

Lord of the Dance

Isn't it paradoxical that with destruction all around and the world on fire, the most appropriate thing to do is dance? Our moves are the dance of Siva, whose wild, frolicking pantomime brings everything to being. Perched in a seemingly precarious posture, framed by a scorching halo, with hair untamed, he is "Lord of the Dance."

Siva's dance is his yoga. For eons, his tireless sway produces the world—all life emerges from his creative romp. Yet as much as he is the creator, he too, is the destroyer. All that gets revealed through the swirl of his limbs and the gestures of his hands and feet is annihilated in due time.

Siva, the cosmic dancer, is the embodiment and manifestation of the fundamental energy of the entire universe. His dance is a reminder that creation and destruction are mutual aspects of one being. Off-balance yet unflinchingly steady, wildly in control, Siva dances his paradox. His dance is alternately sublime and terrible, delightful, and horrifying, raucous, and serene. Siva's polarities produce the world, the choreographed the conundrum of the human experience.

Like partners in a dance, like inseparable twins, creation and destruction go together. Siva's, chaos is his order, his destruction is equal to his liberation. Whether we realize it or not, each of us moves in rhythm to this tireless dance. In the fire ring of your life now, what is being created and what is being torn down? Consider that each day is a kind of dance; you move with your partner (sometimes leading, sometimes following), whirl through the rooms of your home and run errands in town, all the while keeping time to an inner rhythm.

While we keep pace to an invisible choreography, the life-dance we lead is a trial by fire at the brink of birth and death, gain and loss. This dance is gymnastic, requiring agility, strength, and concentration. It is a tricky balancing act where we routinely stumble and then find our way back to center. So, when you wake up in the morning, prepare to participate whole-heartedly in the dance. Make your limbs supple and your mind clear and welcome the crazy, divine whirl of your life.

The Spark of Death

Once, I thought I knew
the way of the world,
young and so far away from my death.
Pangs of yearning grip me still,
in the desert canyon, where light is scarce and
the cracks in the granite smell like rain,
where the archangel wrestled Jacob to the ground,
twisted his sacrum and installed the love of fear inside.

Now death takes me to her cradle and begins to rock me.
Lulled by the sway of years passing
I have been in love with
every song, every train, every storm cloud.
But tonight the glitter of stars in the night sky beckons:

"Empty your pockets, hand in your papers,
disclose your secrets, for the time has come
to let the light of death sparkle your soul."

It's then that a bolt streaks through my cranial cavity,
zigzags wildly down my spine,
and shimmers under my skin
brilliant as beads of turquoise.

A strange silence overtakes me
and everything stands still
like a horse back in the barn after a long run.
I feel a final twitch and quiver
—right smack in the center of my spine—
like aspen leaves
quaking tremulous,
in currents of invisible air.

I Remember This Feeling

I remember this feeling from way back when
as a child looking up under the grand maple in the backyard
and the feeling of my grandmother's pearly skin against mine.
Now it comes back to me in a shimmer,
like a gust of light rippling over the water
swooping through my spine in a tremor
—atmospheric, cathartic, free.

It is not about getting back to where you once were
or striving on toward some distant destination,
rather it is about remembering
who you are and always have been.

Moment by moment, breath by breath
come back to your senses.
Allow grace to flow through you—
lighting up your eye,
humming in your ear,
flickering across your skin.

Open to the ways of the miraculous
by letting the life breath wash over you—
each droplet of prana bearing
the signature imprint of the ancient ones.

Rinse and cleanse
the ten thousand threads,
in your web of connective tissue,
vast as mycelium.
Breathe in the morning mist,
let it oxygenate your blood
and circulate through every fiber of your being.

December Full Moon

Bald head peeks
over the pine crested ridge
how slow its birth!
One one-thousand, two one-thousand,
three one-thousand, four...
the crown emerges,
how fast the world spins!

The Zen of Oz

It all started when Toto pulled back the curtain and revealed nothing but a puny man pulling on his levers. It was a very Zen moment —the bald head, the long black coat, the no God. After the trauma, getting banged on the head and spun around dizzy, the promise is that you too can drop down into a land full of color. The journey is replete with frights, wicked schemes, upside-down moments, and plenty of quirky characters.

It's all a reminder that you need not go to some exotic land to find what you've had all along. Aren't we all too preoccupied with getting to some big prize at the end of the long and winding road? Realize that the whole ordeal is like a movie, a dream, a sleight of hand. The old texts have made this clear since time immemorial. Most people keep falling asleep, lulled by the drug of the day. Should you feel that the great and powerful is outside of yourself you are instantly lost, caught up in monkey mind.

When you realize there is no great and powerful Oz behind the curtain, no single solitary god at the helm, you can be with each glorious thing. You can let yourself be found by the world. Take courage that you need not travel to some far-flung land, you need not even leave your house, but only be in the place you are now, and have always been.

AIR

Savasana II

After sound, listen to silence,
the empty resonance
that echoes and reverberates
—endlessly—
as the thrum of your heart,
the murmur of your breath,
and the sonic swoosh of your blood.

Make your restless body still,
for in stillness the entire world is at peace and in place.
Drop your belief
in a separate self
so that your bones blend into the one body—
the ground below, the sky above, and everything in-between.

Savor the Silence

Savor the silence today
let it settle into your ear
like fresh fallen snow at midnight,
or the echo of a distant train.
Let wisps of thought remind you of silence
the way cirrus clouds sweep the sky at dawn.

You need not conjure silence
it is always here… now…
may it protect you from the
engine of your own craving,
the clang and clatter of
wanting anything more, or less.

Let every sound —the whoosh of the wind,
the hum of the fridge, the din of traffic—
be a soundless echo
—oceanic, tympanic—
murmuring through your blood stream.

Like a lover toward her beloved,
supplicate to the silence
feel it soak right through your skin.
Enter the blood womb of silence
let it pulse in the vestibule of your ears,
nourishing and incubating your soul.

"Silence" wrote Melville, "is the only Voice of our God,"
the unspoken language,
the one common tongue,
that resounds through all space and time.

Let yourself be engulfed by
this immeasurable silence,
let it take you in its wide arms and cradle you
weighty and invisible,
immense beyond reckoning.

Call of Solitude

There is nothing as treasured as a dear friend, someone to be with in idle moments, walking the paths, sharing warbling thoughts, drinking tea. This friend is a confidant, one in whom you can place your trust, convey your love, and know as a virtual friend in God. In Sanskrit the cherished one is *suhrid*, "good of heart," the one who brings you out of yourself, the one who teaches you how to belong. Yet this friend will never show his face or reveal her name, being not of this world, exactly. Only when you are cocooned in solitude, raw within yourself, unguarded and approachable, may the intimate one be revealed and only then, ghostly, like mist.

In the smallest hour, permit a swell of silence to wash over you. Free from the clack and drone of daily doings, you may encounter the friend. Search for her. Sweep your body like a metal detector over hallowed ground. There will come a moment when the vibration quickens, your breath heaves and a current of electricity enters you. This is the time when the treasure of the friend is revealed. With great affection, condense all time and space down to the union between you and yours. Swaddled in togetherness you are be-loved. There, let your heart tremble in joy, unimaginable.

On this great ground of solitude you are changed, in the moment, final. Never lost, nor alone. Intimate, never to be divided, stand in the merciful good and make a silent pact never to leave.

The Whisper of God

It is as difficult to understand prana
as it is to explain God.
The very air we breathe is invisible,
the sanctum of our soul concealed.
O magnum mysterium!
Here the atmosphere is gossamer-thin
rarefied and sheer,
like the brushstroke of breath in your nostrils
and the taste of the finest wine on your tongue.

Drop every last particle of wanting to know,
having to know, needing to know.
Be in the light of the now—
consecrate the space within.
Can you hear God's whisper?

"I am in you always
and have been
since the beginning of time.
The vapor of your breath
the mirror of your mind
the love in your heart are mine."

Heed the Call

To be drawn to a lifetime of practice, one must feel a deep calling inside to be free from pettiness and doubt and the stickiness of a mind that clings. For many, the calling remains muffled or mute, voiceless, stuck in the recess of their throat. It may lie dormant for weeks, months, maybe years, until one day you feel a burning impulse to know it, to heed its command, and to live your life in accord with the inner yearning. This calling prompts you to go to the mat, twist the sinews of your spine, intone strange prayers, and stay up late watching the moon rise.

It is a voice of longing, of passion, an invocation to heal your ailing heart and be in the world without refusal. It is what Mahatma Gandhi once called, "the still small voice inside." This voice may get snuffed out by other voices clamoring in your ear, prompting you to follow their lead and become what they ask of you. Other voices lure you toward a life of commodification, seducing you to seek fulfillment in a world gone mad with materialism. Other voices may confuse you, find fault with who you are, and say you are not good enough. Or the estranged voice may put you down and make you feel an inch tall.

The question is, can you cut through the noise and listen to the still small voice inside, to learn to trust it as your counsellor, your guide, your guru? The yearning, the ardor, works like magnetic attraction. It is a force that beckons by way of invisible charge, in the way that gravity holds everything to the ground. When you follow this inner bidding, you follow a calling to not take the easy way out, but to live by what you feel is true.

It takes trust and courage to heed the voice that summons. You need not resist it or cling to it, but rather only belong to it. Each day when you stretch your fascia, lengthen your spine, and release the grip of your nerves, yield to its presence. If you trust the voice that speaks on behalf of greatness, the voice that coaxes you out of doubt and mistrust and guides you to remember that you are inseparable from the abundance all around you, then follow that voice devotedly to the end of time.

The Breather's Breath

The breather's breath hangs in the
clouds over the mountain ridge,
blasts as sea spray over Pulpit Rock,
and gurgles as molten fire in the earth's center.
The breather's breath courses
through the veins of the sealion and
opens the wings of the swallowtail in flight.
It seeps through the curl of the fiddle head fern and
oozes in the sap of the bristle cone pine.

And listen! The echo of the breather's breath is nearby—
in the wind at the top of the tall pines,
in the patter of rain on the roof,
in the raucous sound of the raven calling,
"caw, caw, caw."

In my youth, brazen and blind, I once thought I could control you,
guide your every passage,
manipulate your flow, restrain your power.
Studying the old anatomical texts,
I once thought I could know your name.

Now the color is waning in the Western sky
and the day exhales its last light.
Shawl over my shoulders, sitting bones down,
I attend to the great mystery
and settle into the breather's breath,
a 10,000-year-old wind
that never comes and goes.

This Very Moment

What we are looking for is not miles down the road
in the future waiting for us to arrive.
Rather it is the immediacy of this very moment—
the split-second swoosh of the calligrapher's pen,
the delighted shriek of the six-month-old,
the streak of lightening in the Western sky.
The true art of living is spontaneity,
perfectly unplanned.

Unfetter the shackles that constrain you,
untame your breath,
let the gusty winds of prana
lift you up like a raptor catching a thermal on high.
There is no way of going back to the old trudge,
quantifying every move, calculating every mile.
You must forge on like a seventeenth-century explorer
into the wild frontier of this very moment,
always new, eternally fresh,
never before arisen.

Each day holds open the gate of the world for you.
You need only drop the burden of expectation from your
shoulders and leave your luggage at the door.

In this very moment
you are summoned to trust more,
to widen the horizon of your heart,
and ready yourself for the next big breath
that may swoop in
and lift you up on its back
like the ancient wind horse,
bearing thunderbolts in the sky.

The Spirit of Repetition

In order to slice through the cobwebs of delusion, you must return to the mat over and over again. If not, unseen forces, tacky and tenuous, may stick to your moods, hem in your heart, and glom onto your dreams. Like wielding a machete, you must slice through the strands of cobwebs that trap you in their tacky net. The best way to do this is to become established in the spirit of repetition.

The spirit of repetition is steady practice, one that sets up a groove of affirmation, a kind of pathway of positivity. At the beginning, this positive groove helps you to be free from entangled thoughts, confusion, blame, grudge-holding, and the like. It helps unfasten the knots that bind. The practice starts at home — loosening your diaphragm, expanding your nerves, dispelling the ghosts of old traumas.

The spirit of repetition involves putting kindness into practice, especially toward the people you live with and who care for you the most. You must keep your third eye open, because division and animosity can creep into relations with the ones you love. Mindfulness is necessary to slice through the invisible film of stickiness that causes rigidity, defensiveness, and self-righteousness. Persevere, as the sticky layers may have been gumming up inside you for many years, if not many lifetimes.

Each time you get to the mat, build a greater capacity for receptivity and care. However, know that the effects of the spirit of repetition are largely invisible. Change is slow to come by. You won't suddenly feel liberated from the icky, grippy layers that hold you down. It takes time, many years, to disentangle the cobwebs of delusion and confusion. This is why you need the spirit of repetition. Trust that the practice has its own alchemy, its own way of changing the chemical signature of "you." Remember, the spirit of repetition has been kept alive for hundreds of years by innumerable followers that have preceded you on this path. When you practice, you take your place in the way of the ancestors —you breathe their same breath, you walk their same walk.

Like time-release medicine, if you are constant in practice, the practice will work on you. When you step onto your mat each day, when you lift, stretch, turn, and lengthen, when you slow the torrent of racing thoughts, know that the spirit of repetition moves through you.

The Spirit of Play

All life begins in a spirit of play. In the mythology of India, the gods, bored to death with their own enlightenment, conjure endless varieties of human drama for their entertainment. Every scenario, every circumstance, every human interaction, is a manifestation of the divine sport of the gods.

Life itself begins in play. Free of responsibility, children are spirited and carefree. Children have time to horse around, toy with things, do stuff "for the hell of it." Krishna, the celebrated child-God of India, knows this best. He romps through the forest, light-hearted and untroubled. He fools around with his brother, fondles the milkmaid's breasts, and finds sport in conquering the terrible demons that lurk in the forest. Krishna's frivolity is an expression of his enlightened nature. By contrast, we typically think of enlightenment as some transcendental, supercalifragilistic state —a kind of high-stakes wisdom. But what if enlightenment is simply play-acting and, like sport, a kind of amusement? In the mythos of the yoga tradition, play connects us to *lila*, the divine foolery of the gods.

The point of play is that it makes the world appear less solid. In play-acting we make things up, we improvise and imagine. We bend notions of what is real. Play, by necessity, is always overflowing, spilling outside the boundaries of reason and determination, blurring the lines of what is right or wrong, good or bad. Play rides the edge between chaos and control. All play is an expression of the raw, unfiltered energy (*shakti*) that is the creative impulse of the gods.

However, there is no way to "practice" play. It comes unscheduled, in the moment, without thinking. It is a spontaneous expression of the inspired and creative force that moves continuously through the world. So each day, loosen the grip that holds you to the "real." Be mischievous, childlike, and fun-loving. Come to embody the spirit of play and in so doing, participate in the delight of the gods.

No Separation

I am riding a stream of breath, solitary,
watching the ups and downs of perpetual flow.
It's going along fine,
as it always does, until everything suddenly stands still
like a seed pod in mid-air, hanging on nothing.
Quotidian, magical,
like a child sighing in her sleep
then rolling to her side
swallowing with a soft smack of her tongue.
It is a moment beyond reckoning,
beyond reason,
stupendous and tender.

Go to the liminal place
—the gap—
between back and front, right and left,
inhale and exhale,
upside and down.
In the end, it's all about letting go and
relinquishing your clasp,
like an escaped helium balloon
aloft inside your chest.

In a moment of suspense,
hover in the staggering silence
—weightless in time—
no separation
between the outside and the in.

The Trap of Entitlement

In times of trial how can we rekindle an essential gratitude for the remarkable gift of this precious human life? Unfortunately, in times of struggle, it is all too common for people to kick into survival mode. Citizens become self-serving, righteous, indignant, and nationalistic. Mindful speech, mindful action, and basic concern for each other go right out the window. Rather than feeling grateful, people are prone to feeling entitled —entitled to land, wealth, guns, and the 5G mindset, "I always should get a signal." Along with the privilege to put up anything and everything on the internet, these are deemed to be God-given rights. Today, people feel entitled to be entertained on their private handheld devices, anytime, anywhere.

The trap of entitlement has been cautioned against for thousands of years. In the Yoga Sutras, non-grasping is one of the foundational tenets of right conduct. Grasping, self-righteousness, and self-deservedness have an obsessive quality. Greed is one of the deadly poisons that infects the mind. In Buddhism, the three toxic afflictions —greed, delusion, and hatred— are colorfully illustrated as the rooster, pig, and the snake. When I assume a kind of entitlement, convinced that the world should serve me, I am self-important, piggish, and prideful. A yoga practice is an antidote to these heart-mind toxins, ushering in attitudes of altruism, understanding, and generosity.

The Zen master Linji once asked his students, "Who is the true person of no title?" When we have humility, when we stop assuming we are entitled to everything, we take our place in the wonder of things. The "true person of no title" does not assume that the world owes him anything but only that he belongs to it.

SPACE

In the Space Between

At long last I have come back to myself
after years of wandering
down vacant hallways, up back stairwells
and across stretches of lonely highway.
I have scrolled through endless pages
sending and receiving
caught in a web of searching.
I have been tossed to and fro,
between gain and loss, love and hate, hope and despair.

Now I return to the seemingly simplest thing,
sitting upright, not moving a muscle,
letting my breath breathe me.
This goes against every urge,
every impulse I have ever known.
All my ploys—
my desire to please you,
to appear witty and charming,
to convince you of my significance,
to get one up on the world—
are for naught.

Helpless, I drop the weighty load of me
and sit bare naked
before the great silence.
Tender-hearted,
I settle into the space between breaths
where joy and sorrow meet.

Consecrate the Space Within

Each day, the most profound and nutritive thing you can do is rest in a space that is wide-open, silent and still. In meditation, as you come into the temple of your body-mind, make your breath tactile, sense the weight of your bones and learn to drop in. Relinquish all urgency. Loosen your sense of time. Mostly what you need is tenderness and a willingness to welcome into your heart that which can never be seen with the naked eye.

Don't insist, banging on the door clamoring to get in. For entry is always given when you least expect it. Be solidly patient and stay true to your calling. Suddenly, invisible like the wind, you will slip past the threshold and enter the sanctum of serenity. It is like walking into a cathedral where many before you have gone to consider, seek solace and pray. Go and sit in the half light, empty of need, not looking to get anywhere or gain anything. Sit in wonder, wide in the open air.

Deflate any doubts that keep you from yourself. Unfetter the knots that bind you to fear and loathing. Be kind toward the small shy you that resides in your heart, the one that longs to be entire, undivided, and free. Bask in the shaft of light that spills from the highest window. Let all the particles of prana settle in your open space of wonder. Consecrate the space within.

Circular Breathing

In practice this morning,
a swoosh of sensation seizes me,
and in a split-second,
I am in a kind of free fall,
like a child on a Ferris wheel,
sinking and soaring,
terrified and titillated
as gravity streaks through my spine.
It brings both
dread and delight
akin to the very first breath
after nine months incubating in the
porous and pulpy womb—
knowing neither up nor down,
side to side, inside or out.

It is then that something untold rushes in
to fill the crater of my being
carved out long ago from the impact of some trauma.
It's as if my body takes the form of a question mark,
curved and linear, with a dot at the end.

Can I learn not to grasp
at straws or stars
and travel like a red blood cell
living but 120 days?

The Buddha taught that
all things appear like lightening, dewdrops,
and bubbles on a fast-moving stream.
Birth, old age, sickness, and death
are the hallmarks of *samsara*
and craving the glue that binds.

On the way down, I realize I do not need
the thing I sought for so long,
and surrender to an unintelligible thing,
a perpetual presence,
that never lives nor dies.
It is like circular breathing,
where the notes played are not different
from the freshness of the air inhaled.

Giant Earplugs

The mountains this morning
are giant earplugs
deafening all sound
in the canyon of my mind.

The sky is thin
but a sheet of glass
reflecting back to me
the pitter-patter of my thoughts.
Ozone.

Where the Infinite and the Finite Meet

As you walk through your day, connect to the immediate, changing needs of the moment and at the same time yoke to the Great Source all around. If your life is anything like mine, your days are filled to the brim —sending and receiving, getting your nine-year-old on the bus for school, taking care of aging parents, making your tahini toast in the morning. Life is always a bustling stream of activity, don't you find? Take each thing as it comes and learn to grow old. Do not reject the world nor cling to it.

Sometimes we push the world away thinking, "oh, this is not right, this is no good, this doesn't belong here!" At other times we hold on for dear life, clinging to people, places, and things. Fifty percent of practice is just bearing witness to the sometimes turbulent, sometimes serene ways of the world.

When we forget the Great Source —the unlimited, omnipresent, mother of all things— we get thrown into a tizzy. You must know the *tizzy-asana*, where you spin like a top, wobble around, and everything goes out of kilter. Can you stay connected to the Great Source while meeting full-heartedly the moment at hand? Can you be of the earth —imminent, time-bound and limited, and at the same time be of the sky— formless, unlimited, and transcendent? The challenge then, now, is to do a kind of double move —like the two-step dance— where you engage and let go at the same time. Don't hold too tight or too loose. If you hold too tightly, you will squeeze the moment. If your hold is too lax, you'll never make the connection.

This practice is full of paradox, where you are both child and elder, matter and spirit, the wise one and the fool. Allow the timeless to move through you while dealing with each passing thing. In the shuffle of your daily round, know the eternal to be right at hand, intimate, nearer to you than your ideas, thoughts, or opinions. Let your practice guide you smack dab into the middle of the moment, where the infinite and the finite meet.

Silent Sky

    silent sky
    mountain skirts
    magpie gang
    cracks loudly

Believe in Nothing

Shunryu Suzuki, celebrated author of *Zen Mind Beginner's Mind*, once said, "I believe it is necessary, absolutely necessary to believe in nothing, that is we have to believe in something that has no form and no color —something which exists before all forms and colors appear." That is radical if not ridiculous. How can you believe in something that is nothing, naught, zero? The famed Danish philosopher Soren Kierkegaard spoke of faith as a paradox, an absurdity. Surely belief in nothing is absurd. Yet it lies at the very heart of practice. It is something you should put your whole self into and practice diligently every day. Faith by necessity is irrational. It exists outside the calibrations of the conceptual mind. In fact, faith begins the moment thought stops. Placing faith in the formless goes far beyond common sense.

When it comes to nothing, people get confused. They think nothing is *nada*, vacant, void, like a black hole. But nothing is like garden soil —rich and fertile. You can grow anything in that soil! All that you do —your plans, your projects, raising a family— are cultivated in the bountiful soil of zilch. It takes time to get a sense for how nothing gives rise to everything, the way that silence gives way to sound. So, spend time in the formless and till the soil of nothingness. Put your whole-hearted conviction into the abundance of emptiness. Know it to be the mother of all things.

Tent Top

    Flags
    on the tent top
               flop.

    Flip flap,
        flip flap,
               Ho!

Black Crow

Black crow atop the tall pine calls,
"caw," "caw," "caw"
—going hoarse—
"listen to the dharma!"
"listen to the dharma!"

Kudos to the Unspeakable

I don't want to talk your ear off because at some level language always falls short, or spills over, like late night cable television. For this reason, many spiritual teachers don't use language at all, but transmit their teaching through a simple hand gesture, a look, a shout, or by simply shutting up and not saying a word. For instance, in the celebrated "Flower Sermon," the time-honored Buddha transmitted a wordless sermon to his followers by raising a white flower. Indian gurus are known to impart *shakti-pat* —a kind of psychic blast to wake up their students —and Zen masters are famous for whacking disciples on the back.

It is not only the Big East gurus who point to the inexplicable, using little to no language. The French philosopher Emmanuel Levinas, a Jew who survived the Holocaust as a prisoner of war, pointed to the linguistically simple, *il y a*. Translated roughly as "there it is," or "there goes," this phrase points to the strange wonder of that which is both evident and inexplicable. But this, too, may be just more language.

The cornerstone of all Zen koans begins with the question, "Does a dog have Buddha nature?" The celebrated master Joshu responds emphatically, "Mu." It is an inexplicable reply, a mono-syllabic utterance not dissimilar from the guttural blurt of a bovine, that nevertheless points to the essential nature of all things. In zazen, mu is used like a mantra, inseparable from the breath.

The best way to commune with the ineffable is to sit still and shush up. Sitting in noble silence on your cushion is an invitation to let all the text, all the chit-chatting and snap-chatting come to rest. And you don't need to go to Rishikesh or Santa Fe to find it. That which escapes language is always available, in the space between the words you read here, in the gap between breaths, in the silence after sound. Here it is! *Il y a!* Welcome the unspeakable by letting yourself slip through the cracks in language. The greatest wisdom is inconceivable. So, spend time each day in a hush of silence, communing in the stillness between thoughts. I will meet you in the space of wordless wonder, beyond reckoning, an anonymous space that is always right before your eyes, boundless and bright.

End of the Year

The year got under our skin—
the bugs, the lies, the scorched earth
and many times I felt
a shadow of doubt creep over me.

This year there were 10,000 deaths
and we each felt the ache of loss,
mourning in private
through the surging days.

The end of the year
is the time to melt,
to absolve the woes of despair and
attend to the fire within
that dances and shimmers
like phosphorescent sparks,
or crystals on fresh fallen snow.

Look at the beauty all around!
The girl with the yellow ribbon in her hair,
the winter's light on the canyon wall,
the peace of the sleeping child.

Today the pulse of prana moves through me
and I feel each breath as a new beginning.
I reach out through this undying space to touch you
and feel you reach back, touching me.

Our bond, our belonging sustains us.
May we remember that each of us is a gift
and in the year that lies ahead,
our vow, our longing, our dream,
is to be the gift that keeps on giving.

It's This Simple

Each day is as simple as this:
wake up and sit
mind your step
tend the garden
walk in the hill country
laugh over dinner
sleep with the blinds down.

Be As You Are

It's funny how we spend an entire lifetime trying to get somewhere. We struggle to get ahead in life, to make the grade, to get the big contract, to be liked on social media. A spiritual discipline is not immune to the mind that grasps. We try to get better at yoga, become more mindful, improve our meditation. While these are worthy goals, they are actually a big problem.

More often than not, trying to better ourselves only blocks progress on the path. Again and again, we fail to realize that the goal is to simply be. Always busy and on demand, we are no longer a collective of human beings, but rather "human doers." For this reason, you should never "do yoga," but "be yoga." What does it mean to just **be**? And how do we put it into practice? Follow the example of trees. And clouds and crayfish. Follow the example of your four-legged friend waiting at the door to go out in the morning.

Being is simple, straightforward. When a monk asks the heavyweight Zen master Joshu, "What is the meaning of the first patriarch coming from the West?" (that is to say, what is the meaning of this entire practice), Joshu responds, "The oak tree in the garden."

It is hard to appreciate just being. Eternally restless and hankering for more, we distract ourselves with our phones, busy ourselves with to-do lists, pang for more likes on Instagram, and strive to be good. Again and again, we keep busy, while falling prey to the belief that we need to be other than we are.

To be, requires stripping away, going bare bones. This is referred to in Christian doctrine as "fasting of the heart." In yoga, it is called *sat-chit-ananda*, "the joy of simply being aware." Sadly, we feel that we are never enough. We keep wanting more...more attention, more money, more hits, more followers, more self-knowledge, more peace.

Can we cease our craving and realize we already have enough? Can we relish in just being? *Tat tvam asi.* You are being. Or put another way, be as you are. When we accept that to be is enough, then we need not go anywhere or get anything. When we have nothing more to gain and nothing more to lose, then finally, at last, we are content to be with what is.

Feast Today

Feast today on simple things—
the chalk-colored sky at dawn,
the face of a loved one teleported from far away,
the newspaper article about the couple that lived 66 years together
and then died days apart.

Feast on the memories of your father's broad shoulders
and your grandmother's wrinkled hands, skin delicate as pearl.
Bring on the bread, bring the wine.
Welcome all the tastes —sour, bitter, and sweet.
Savor a song, savor your breath.
Feast today on this remarkable life,
this wild, abundant, unfathomable life.

Sit. Eat. Say a short prayer (nothing fancy)
for the benefit of all beings—
great and small.

Give thanks to the giver
whose gift keeps on giving.
Listen to the whir of the November wind
and whisper the simplest invocation,
indistinguishable from breath itself,
"amen."

In Gratitude

I wish to extend my kindest thanks to the many eyes who helped shape, edit, and define this collection. I extend bunches of gratitude to Courtney Zenner and Kim Schwab for their careful editorial eyes. I am grateful for Cristina Dispigno for her ever-present support in the execution of this project and all things Prajna. For all touches concerning the graphic design of this book —I wish to extend many thanks to the dedicated yogini Patricia Cousins. I am eternally grateful for the care and expert handling that my wife Surya has given to this project. Last, but not least, I give thanks to my son Eno Little for his fine eye in taking the cover photographs.